'HE NEEDED TO HEAR AFRICA SPEAK FOR ITSELF AFTER A LIFETIME OF HEARING AFRICA SPOKEN ABOUT BY OTHERS.'

D1471555

CHINUA ACHEBE
Born 1930, Ogidi, Anambra, Nigeria
Died 2013, Boston, Massachusetts, USA

'What is Nigeria to Me?' is adapted from a speech given at the
Nigerian Institute of International Affairs in Lagos in 2008.
'Travelling White' was originally published in the *Guardian* in
1989, and 'Africa's Tarnished Name' in *Another Africa* in 1998.
'Africa is People' is adapted from a speech delivered at the
Organization for Economic Co-operation and Development
in Paris in 1998. All are included in *The Education of a
British-Protected Child* (2011).

ACHEBE IN PENGUIN MODERN CLASSICS
Anthills of the Savannah
Arrow of God
The Education of a British-Protected child
A Man of the People
No Longer at Ease
There was a Country
Things Fall Apart

CHINUA ACHEBE

Africa's Tarnished Name

PENGUIN BOOKS

PENGUIN CLASSICS

UK | USA | Canada | Ireland | Australia
India | New Zealand | South Africa

Penguin Books is part of the Penguin Random House group
of companies whose addresses can be found at
global.penguinrandomhouse.com.

Penguin
Random House
UK

This selection first published 2018

010

Copyright © Chinua Achebe, 2009

Set in 11.2/13.75 pt Dante MT Std
Typeset by Jouve (UK), Milton Keynes
Printed and bound in Great Britain by Clays Ltd, Elcograf S.p.A.

ISBN: 978-0-241-33883-4

www.greenpenguin.co.uk

MIX
Paper from
responsible sources
FSC
www.fsc.org   FSC® C018179

Penguin Random House is committed to a
sustainable future for our business, our readers
and our planet. This book is made from Forest
Stewardship Council® certified paper.

Contents

What Is Nigeria to Me?

Nigerian nationality was for me and my generation an acquired taste – like cheese. Or better still, like *ballroom* dancing. Not dancing *per se*, for that came naturally; but this titillating version of slow-slow-quick-quick-slow performed in close body contact with a female against a strange, elusive beat. I found, however, that once I had overcome my initial awkwardness I could do it pretty well.

Perhaps these irreverent analogies would only occur to someone like me, born into a strongly multiethnic, multilingual, multireligious, somewhat chaotic colonial situation. The first passport I ever carried described me as a 'British Protected Person', an unexciting identity embodied in a phrase that no one was likely to die for. I don't mean it was entirely devoid of emotive meaning. After all, 'British' meant you were located somewhere in the flaming red portion of the world map that covered a quarter of the entire globe in those days and was called 'the British Empire, where the sun never sets'. It had a good ring to it in my childhood ears – a magical fraternity, vague but vicariously glorious.

But I am jumping ahead of myself. My earliest awareness in the town of Ogidi did not include any of that British stuff, nor indeed the Nigerian stuff. That came with progress in school. Ogidi is one of a thousand or more 'towns' that make up the Igbo nation, one of Nigeria's (indeed Africa's) largest ethnic groups. But the Igbo, numbering over ten million, are a curious 'nation'. They have been called names like 'stateless' or 'acephalous' by anthropologists; 'argumentative' by those sent to administer them. But what the Igbo are is not the negative suggested by such descriptions but strongly, positively, in favor of small-scale political organization so that (as they would say) every man's eye would reach where things are happening. So every one of the thousand towns was a mini state with complete jurisdiction over its affairs. A sense of civic attachment to their numerous towns was more real for precolonial Igbo people than any unitary pan-Igbo feeling. This made them notoriously difficult to govern centrally, as the British discovered but never appreciated nor quite forgave. Their dislike was demonstrated during the Biafran tragedy, when they accused the Igbo of threatening to break up a nation-state they had carefully and laboriously put together.

The paradox of Biafra was that the Igbo themselves had originally championed the Nigerian nation more spiritedly than other Nigerians. One proof of this: the British had thrown more of them into jail for sedition than any others during the two decades or so of pre-independence agitation and troublemaking. So the Igbo were second to none on the nationalist front when Britain finally conceded independence to Nigeria in 1960, a move that, in retrospect, seems like a masterstroke of tactical withdrawal to achieve a supreme strategic advantage.

At the time we were proud of what we had just achieved. True, Ghana had beaten us to it by three years, but then Ghana was a tiny affair, easy to manage, compared to the huge lumbering giant called Nigeria. We did not have to be vociferous like Ghana; just our presence was enough. Indeed, the elephant was our national emblem; our airline's was the flying elephant! Nigerian troops soon distinguished themselves in a big way in the United Nations peacekeeping efforts in the Congo. Our elephant, defying aerodynamics, was flying!

Traveling as a Nigerian was exciting. People listened to us. Our money was worth more than the dollar. When the driver of a bus in the British colony of Northern Rhodesia in 1961 asked me what I was doing sitting in the front of the bus, I told him nonchalantly that I was going to Victoria Falls. In amazement he stooped lower and asked where I came from. I replied, even more casually, 'Nigeria, if you must know; and, by the way, in Nigeria we sit where we like in the bus.'

Back home I took up the rather important position of director of external broadcasting, an entirely new radio service aimed primarily at our African neighbors. I could do it in those days, because our politicians were yet to learn the uses of information control and did not immediately attempt to regiment our output. They were learning fast, though. But before I could get enmeshed in that, something much nastier had seized hold of all of us.

The six-year-old Nigerian federation was falling apart from the severe strain of regional animosity and ineffectual central authority. The transparent failure of the electoral process to translate the will of the electorate into recognizable results at the polls led to mass frustration and violence. While Western Nigeria, one of the four regions, was going up literally in flames, the quiet and dignified Nigerian prime minister was hosting a commonwealth conference to extricate Harold Wilson from a mess he had got himself into in faraway Rhodesia. But so tense was the local situation that the visiting heads of government had to be airlifted by helicopter from the Lagos airport into a secluded suburb to avoid rampaging crowds.

Nigeria's first military coup took place even as those dignitaries were flying out of Lagos again at the end of their conference. One of them, Archbishop Makarios of Cyprus, was in fact still in the country.

The prime minister and two regional premiers were killed by the coup-makers. In the bitter, suspicious atmosphere of the time, a naïvely idealistic coup proved a terrible disaster. It was interpreted with plausibility as a plot by the ambitious Igbo of the east to take control of Nigeria from the Hausa-Fulani north. Six months later, northern officers carried out a revenge coup in which they killed Igbo officers and men in large numbers. If it had ended there, the matter might have been seen as a very tragic interlude in nation building, a horrendous tit for tat. But the northerners turned on Igbo civilians living in the north and unleashed waves of brutal massacres, which Colin Legum of *The Observer* was the first to describe as a pogrom. It was estimated that thirty thousand civilian men, women, and children died in these massacres. Igbos were fleeing in hundreds of thousands from all parts of Nigeria to their homeland in the east.

I was one of the last to flee from Lagos. I simply could not bring myself quickly enough to accept that I could no longer live in my nation's capital, although the facts clearly said so. One Sunday morning I was telephoned from Broadcasting House and informed that armed soldiers who appeared drunk had come looking for me to test which was stronger, my pen or their gun!

5

The offence of my pen was that it had written a novel called *A Man of the People,* a bitter satire on political corruption in an African country that resembled Nigeria. I wanted the novel to be a denunciation of the kind of independence we were experiencing in postcolonial Nigeria and many other countries in the 1960s, and I intended it to scare my countrymen into good behavior with a frightening cautionary tale. The best monster I could come up with was a military coup d'etat, which every sane Nigerian at the time knew was rather far-fetched! But life and art had got so entangled that season that the publication of the novel, and Nigeria's first military coup, happened within two days of each other.

Critics abroad called me a prophet, but some of my countrymen saw it differently: my novel was proof of my complicity in the first coup.

I was very lucky that Sunday morning. The drunken soldiers, after leaving Broadcasting House, went to a residence I had recently vacated. Meanwhile I was able to take my wife and two little children into hiding, from where I finally sent them to my ancestral home in Eastern Nigeria. A week or two later, unknown callers asked for me on the telephone in my hideout. My host denied my presence. It was time then to leave Lagos.

My feeling towards Nigeria was one of profound disappointment. Not because mobs were hunting down and killing in the most savage manner innocent civilians in many parts of northern Nigeria, but because the federal government sat by and let it happen. The final consequence of this failure of the state to fulfill its primary obligation to its citizens was the secession of Eastern Nigeria as the Republic of Biafra. The demise of Nigeria at that point was averted only by Britain's spirited diplomatic and military support of its model colony. It was Britain and the Soviet Union which together crushed the upstart Biafran state. At the end of the thirty-month war, Biafra was a vast smoldering rubble. The cost in human lives was a staggering two million souls, making it one of the bloodiest civil wars in human history.

I found it difficult to forgive Nigeria and my countrymen and -women for the political nonchalance and cruelty that unleashed upon us these terrible events, which set us back a whole generation and robbed us of the chance, clearly within our grasp, to become a medium-rank developed nation in the twentieth century.

My immediate response was to leave Nigeria at the end of the war, having honorably, I hoped, stayed around long enough to receive whatever retribution might be due to me for renouncing Nigeria for thirty months. Fortunately the federal government proclaimed a general amnesty, and the only punishment I received was the general financial and emotional indemnity that war losers pay, and some relatively minor personal harassment. I went abroad to New England (no irony intended), to the University of Massachusetts at Amherst, and stayed four years and then another year at the University of Connecticut. It was by far my longest exile ever from Nigeria and it gave me time to reflect and to heal somewhat. Without setting out consciously to do so, I was redefining my relationship to Nigeria. I realized that I could not reject her, but neither could it be business as usual. What was Nigeria to me?

Our 1960 national anthem, given to us as a parting gift by a British housewife in England, had called Nigeria 'our sovereign motherland'. The current anthem, put together by a committee of Nigerian intellectuals and actually worse than the first one, invokes the father image. But it has occurred to me that Nigeria is neither my mother nor my father. Nigeria is a child. Gifted, enormously talented, prodigiously endowed, and incredibly wayward.

Being a Nigerian is abysmally frustrating and unbelievably exciting. I have said somewhere that in my next reincarnation I want to be a Nigerian again; but I have also, in a rather angry book called *The Trouble with Nigeria*, dismissed Nigerian travel advertisements with the suggestion that only a tourist with a kinky addiction to self-flagellation would pick Nigeria for a holiday. And I mean both.

Nigeria needs help. Nigerians have their work cut out for them – to coax this unruly child along the path of useful creative development. We are the *parents* of Nigeria, not vice versa. A generation will come, if we do our work patiently and well – and given luck – a generation that will call Nigeria father or mother. But not yet.

Meanwhile our present work is not entirely without its blessing and reward. This wayward child can show now and again great intimations of affection. I have seen this flow towards me at certain critical moments.

When I was in America after the Biafran war, an army officer who sat on the council of my university in Nigeria as representative of the federal military government pressured the university to call me back home. This officer had fought in the field against my fellow Biafrans during the civil war and had been seriously wounded. He had every right to be bitter against people like me. I had never met him, but he knew my work and was himself a poet.

More recently, after a motor accident in 2001 that left me with serious injuries, I have witnessed an outflow of affection from Nigerians at every level. I am still totally dumbfounded by it. The hard words Nigeria and I have said to each other begin to look like words of anxious love, not hate. Nigeria is a country where nobody can wake up in the morning and ask: what can I do now? There is work for all.

2008

Traveling White

In October 1960, I enjoyed the first important perk of my writing career: I was awarded a Rockefeller Fellowship to travel for six months anywhere I chose in Africa. I decided to go to east, central, and southern Africa.

I set out with high hopes and very little knowledge of the real Africa. I visited Kenya, Uganda, Tanganyika, and Zanzibar, and then Northern Rhodesia and Southern Rhodesia. I had had vague notions of going to South-West Africa as well, and even South Africa itself. But Southern Rhodesia proved more than enough for me on that journey and I turned around after a little more than a week there.

The chief problem was racism. The only African country I had visited before was Ghana, the flagship of Africa's independence movement. Ghana had been independent for a few years and was justly the pride of emergent Africa. Nigeria had won her own freedom from Britain just before my journey, on October 1, 1960, and I set forth with one month's worth of ex-colonial confidence – the wind of change, as it were, behind my sails.

The first shock came when we were about to land in Nairobi, and we were handed immigration forms to fill out. After your name, you had to define yourself more fully by filling in one of four boxes: European, Asiatic, Arab, Other! At the airport there were more of the same forms and I took one as a souvenir. I was finding the experience almost funny.

There were other minor incidents, as when the nice matronly British receptionist at the second-class hotel I checked in to in Dar es Salaam told me she didn't mind having Africans in her hotel and remembered a young West African woman who had stayed there a year or so ago and had 'behaved perfectly' all the time she was there and spoke such beautiful English.

I read in the papers that a European Club in Dar was at that time debating whether it ought to amend its rules so that Julius Nyerere, who was then chief minister, might be able to accept the invitation of a member to drink there.

But as the weeks passed, my encounters became less and less amusing. I shall recount just two more, which happened in Rhodesia (modern Zambia and Zimbabwe).

I was met at Salisbury Airport by two young white academics and a black postgraduate student from the new University of Rhodesia. The Rockefeller Foundation, apparently knowing the terrain better than I did, had taken the precaution of enlisting the assistance of these literature teachers to meet me and generally keep an eye on my program. The first item on the agenda was to check in to my hotel. It turned out to be the new five-star Jameson Hotel, which had just been opened in order to avoid such international incidents as the refusal of accommodation to a distinguished countryman of mine, Sir Francis Ibiam, governor of Eastern Nigeria, president of the World Council of Churches, and a British knight!

I was neither a knight, a governor, nor president of any council, but a poor, unknown writer, traveling on the generosity of an enlightened American foundation. This generosity did not, however, stretch so far as to accommodate the kind of bills the Jameson Hotel would present.

But that was another story, which would unfold to me later. For the moment, my three escorts took me to my hotel, where I checked in and then blithely offered them a drink. It was the longest order I had or have ever made. The waiter kept going and then returning with an empty tray and more questions, the long and short of which was that the two bwanas could have their beer and so could I because I was staying in the hotel but the other black fellow could only have coffee. So I called the entire thing off. Southern Rhodesia was simply awful.

Those were not jet days, and my journey home

entailed an overnight stop in Livingstone, Northern Rho-
desia. The manager of the rather nice hotel where I
stayed spotted me at dinner, came over and introduced
himself, and sat at my table for a chat. It was a surprise; I
thought he was coming to eject me. He had been man-
ager of the Ambassador Hotel in Accra, Ghana. From
him I learnt that Victoria Falls was only twenty-odd miles
away and that a bus went there regularly from the hotel.

So the next morning I boarded the bus. From where I
sat – next to the driver's seat – I missed what was going
on in the vehicle. When finally I turned around, probably
because of a certain unnatural silence, I saw with horror
that everyone around me was white. As I had turned
round they had averted their stony gazes, whose hostility
I had felt so palpably at the back of my head. What had
become of all the black people at the bus stop? Why had
no one told me? I looked back again and only then took
in the detail of a partition and a door.

I have often asked myself what I might have done if I
had noticed the separate entrances before I boarded; and
I am not sure.

Anyhow, there I was sitting next to the driver's seat in
a Jim Crow bus in Her Majesty's colony of Northern
Rhodesia, later to be known as Zambia. The driver
(black) came aboard, looked at me with great surprise,
but said nothing.

The ticket collector appeared as soon as the journey got under way. I did not have to look back anymore: my ears were now like two antennae on each side of my head. I heard a bolt move and the man stood before me. Our conversation went something like this:

TICKET COLLECTOR: What are you doing here?
CHINUA ACHEBE: I am traveling to Victoria Falls.
T.C.: Why are you sitting here?
C.A.: Why not?
T.C.: Where do you come from?
C.A.: I don't see what it has to do with it. But if you must know, I come from Nigeria, and there we sit where we like in the bus.

He fled from me as from a man with the plague. My European co-travelers remained as silent as the grave. The journey continued without further incident until we got to the Falls. Then a strange thing happened. The black travelers in the back rushed out in one huge stampede to wait for me at the door and to cheer and sing my praises.

I was not elated. A monumental sadness descended on me. I could be a hero because I was in transit, and these unfortunate people, more brave by far than I, had formed a guard of honor for me!

The awesome waterfall did not revive my spirits. I

walked about wrapped in my raincoat and saw the legendary sight and went back to the terminal and deliberately walked into the front of another bus. And such is the speed of hopeful news in oppressed places that nobody challenged me. And I paid my fare!

And so I never did go to South-West Africa (Namibia) in 1961. And neither did Wolfgang Zeidler twenty-five years later, for very different reasons. It is a curious little story, which came my way in 1988 when I went to lecture at the University of California at Berkeley.

A librarian there showed me a letter she had received from a friend of hers in Germany to whom she had once introduced my book *Things Fall Apart*. This friend, according to the letter, had then loaned the book to his neighbor, who was a distinguished judge. The reason for the loan was that the judge was planning with much enthusiasm to immigrate to Namibia after his retirement and accept the offer made to him to become a constitutional consultant to the Namibian regime. He planned to buy a big farm out there and spend his retirement in the open and pleasant air of the African veldt.

His neighbor, no doubt considering the judge's enthusiasm and optimism rather excessive, if not downright unhealthy, asked him to read *Things Fall Apart* on his flight to or from Namibia. Which he apparently did. The result was dramatic. In the words of the letter shown to me, the judge said that 'he had never seen Africa in that way and that after having read that book he was no more innocent.' And he closed the Namibia chapter.

Elsewhere in the letter, the judge was described as a leading constitutional judge in Germany; as a man with 'the sharpest intelligence'. For about twelve years he had been president of the Bundesverfassungsgericht, the highest constitutional court in Germany. In short, he was the kind of person the South Africans would have done much to have in their corner, a man whose presence in Namibia would give considerable comfort to the regime there. His decision not to go was obviously a triumph of common sense and humanity over stupidity and racial bigotry.

But how was it that this prominent German jurist carried such a blind spot about Africa all his life? Did he never read the papers? Why did he need an African novel to open his eyes? My own theory is that he needed to hear Africa speak for itself after a lifetime of hearing Africa spoken about by others.

I offer the story of the judge, Wolfgang Zeidler, as a companion piece to the fashionable claim made even by writers that literature can do nothing to alter our social and political condition. Of course it can!

1989

Africa's Tarnished Name

It is a great irony of history and geography that Africa, whose landmass is closer than any other to the mainland of Europe, should come to occupy in the European psychological disposition the farthest point of otherness, should indeed become Europe's very antithesis. The French-African poet and statesman Léopold Sédar Senghor, in full awareness of this paradox, chose to celebrate that problematic proximity in a poem, 'Prayer to Masks', with the startling imagery of one of nature's most profound instances of closeness: 'joined together at the navel.' And why not? After all, the shores of northern Africa and southern Europe enclose, like two cupped hands, the waters of the world's most famous sea, perceived by the ancients as the very heart and center of the world. Senghor's metaphor would have been better appreciated in the days of ancient Egypt and Greece than today.

History aside, geography has its own brand of lesson in the paradox of proximity for us. This lesson, which was probably lost on everyone else except those of us living in West Africa in the last days of the British Raj, was the ridiculous fact of longitudinal equality between London, mighty imperial metropolis, and Accra, rude rebel camp of colonial insurrection; so that, their unequal stations in life notwithstanding, they were named by the same Greenwich meridian and consequently doomed together to the same time of day!

But longitude is only half the story. There is also latitude, and latitude gives London and Accra very different experiences of midday temperature, for example, and perhaps gave their inhabitants over past eons of time radically different complexions. So differences are there, if those are what one is looking for. But there is no way in which such differences as do exist could satisfactorily explain the profound perception of alienness which Africa has come to represent for Europe.

This perception problem is not in its origin the result of ignorance, as we are sometimes inclined to think. At least, it is not ignorance entirely, or even primarily. It was in general a deliberate *invention* devised to facilitate two gigantic historical events: the Atlantic slave trade and the colonization of Africa by Europe, the second event following closely on the heels of the first, and the two together stretching across almost half a millennium from about A.D. 1500. In an important and authoritative study of this invention, two American scholars, Dorothy Hammond and Alta Jablow, show how a dramatic change in the content of British writing about Africa coincided with an increase in the volume of the slave trade to its highest level in the eighteenth century. That content

> shifted from almost indifferent and matter-of-fact reports of what the voyagers had seen to judg-mental evaluation of the Africans . . . The shift to such pejorative comment was due in large meas-ure to the effects of the slave trade. A vested interest in the slave trade produced a literature of devaluation, and since the slave trade was under attack, the most derogatory writing about Africa came from its literary defenders. [Scottish slave trader Archibald] Dalzel, for instance, prefaced his work [*The History of Dahomy*] with an apolo-gia for slavery: 'Whatever evils the slave trade may be attended with . . . it is mercy . . . to poor wretches, who . . . would otherwise suffer from the butcher's knife.' Numerous pro-slavery tracts appeared, all intent upon showing the immoral-ity and degradation of Africans . . . Enslavement of such a degraded people was thus not only jus-tifiable but even desirable. The character of Africans could change only for the better through

contact with their European masters. Slavery, in effect, became the means of the Africans' salvation, for it introduced them to Christianity and civilization.[1]

The vast arsenal of derogatory images of Africa amassed to defend the slave trade and, later, colonization gave the world a literary tradition that is now, happily, defunct, but also a particular way of looking (or, rather, not looking) at Africa and Africans that endures, alas, into our own day. And so, although those sensational 'African' novels which were so popular in the nineteenth century and the early part of the twentieth have trickled to a virtual stop, their centuries-old obsession with lurid and degrading stereotypes of Africa has been bequeathed to the cinema, to journalism, to certain varieties of anthropology, even to humanitarianism and missionary work itself.

A few years ago, there was an extraordinary program on television about the children of the major Nazi war criminals, whose lives had been devastated by the burden of the guilt of their fathers. I remember how I felt quite sorry for them in the beginning. But then, out of nowhere, came the information that one of them had gone into the church and would go as a missionary to the Congo. I sat up.

'What has the Congo got to do with it?' I asked my television screen. Then I remembered the motley parade of adventurers, of saints and sinners that had been drawn from Europe to that region since it was first discovered by Europe in 1482 – Franciscan monks, Jesuit priests, envoys from the kings of Portugal, explorers and missionaries, agents of King Leopold of the Belgians, H. M. Stanley, Roger Casement, Joseph Conrad, Albert Schweitzer, ivory hunters and rubber merchants, slave traders and humanitarians. They all made their visit and left their mark, for good or ill. And the Congo, like the ancient tree by the much used farm road, bears on its bark countless scars of the machete.

Paradoxically, a saint like Schweitzer can give one a lot more trouble than a King Leopold II, villain of unmitigated guilt, because along with doing good and saving African lives Schweitzer also managed to announce that the African was indeed his brother, but only his *junior* brother.

But of all the hundreds and thousands of European visitors to the Congo region in the last five hundred years, there were few who had the deftness and sleight of hand of Joseph Conrad, or who left as deep a signature on that roadside tree. In his Congo novella, *Heart of Darkness,* Conrad managed to transform elements from centuries of transparently crude and fanciful writing

21

about Africans into a piece of 'serious' and permanent literature.

Halfway through his story, Conrad describes a journey up the River Congo in the 1890s as though it were the very first encounter between conscious humanity, coming from Europe, and an unconscious, primeval hegemony that had apparently gone nowhere and seen nobody since the world was created. Naturally, it is the conscious party that tells the story:

> We were wanderers on a prehistoric earth, on the earth that wore the aspect of an unknown planet. We could have fancied ourselves the first of men taking possession of an accursed inheritance.[2]

'Prehistoric earth . . . unknown planet . . . fancied ourselves the first of men.'

This passage, which is Conrad at his best, or his worst, according to the reader's predilection, goes on at some length through 'a burst of yells', 'a whirl of black limbs', 'of hands clapping', 'feet stamping', 'bodies swaying', 'eyes rolling', 'black incomprehensible frenzy', 'the prehistoric man himself', 'the night of first ages'. And then Conrad delivers his famous coup de grace. Were these creatures really human? And he answers the question with the most sophisticated ambivalence of double negatives:

No they were not inhuman. Well, you know that
was the worst of it – this suspicion of their not
being inhuman.[3]

But to return to the word 'fancied', which Conrad's
genius had lit upon:

We could have fancied ourselves the first of men
taking possession of an accursed inheritance.

I suggest that 'fancied' is the alarm word insinuated into
Conrad's dangerously highfalutin delirium by his genius
as well as simple reason and sanity, but almost immedi-
ately crowded out, alas, by the emotional and psychological
spell cast on him by the long-established and well-heeled
tradition of writing about Africa. Conrad was at once a
prisoner of this tradition and its most influential pro-
moter, for he, more than anyone else, secured its
admission into the hall of fame of 'canonical' literature.
Fancy, sometimes called Imagination, is not inimical to
Fiction. On the contrary, they are bosom friends. But
they also observe careful protocol around each other's
property and around the homestead of their droll and
difficult neighbor, Fact.

Conrad was a writer who kept much of his fiction
fairly close to the facts of his life as a sailor. He had no
obligation to do so, but that was what he chose to do – to

write about places that actually exist and about people who live in them. He confessed in his 1917 author's note that

> *Heart of Darkness* is experience too, but it is experience pushed a little (and only very little) beyond the actual facts of the case for the perfectly legitimate, I believe, purpose of bringing it home to the minds and bosoms of the readers.[4]

One fact of the case which Conrad may not have known was how much traffic the River Congo had already seen before it saw him in the 1890s. Even if one discounts the Africans who lived on its banks, there had been many Europeans on the river before Conrad. There was a European sailing ship on the Congo four hundred years before he made his journey, and fancied himself the first of men to do it. That degree of fancying needs a good dose of fact to go with it.

The Portuguese captain, Diogo Cão, who discovered the river for Europe in 1482 was actually looking for something else when he stumbled on it; he was looking for a passage around Africa into the Indian Ocean. On his second voyage, he went beyond his first stop up the river and heard from the inhabitants of the area about a powerful ruler whose capital was still farther up. Cao left four Franciscan monks to study the situation and resumed the primary purpose of his expedition. On his way back, he once more detoured into the Congo to pick up his monks; but they were gone! He seized, in retaliation, a number of African hostages, carried them off to Lisbon, and delivered them to King Manuel of Portugal.[5] This unpropitious beginning of Europe's adventure in the heart of Africa was quickly mended when Cao returned to the Congo for the third time in 1487, bringing back his African hostages, who had meanwhile learned the Portuguese language and Christian religion. Cao was taken to see the king, the Mweni-Congo, seated on an ivory throne surrounded by his courtiers. Cão's monks were returned to him, and all was well. An extraordinary period ensued in which the king of Congo became a Christian with the title of Dom Afonso I. Before very long,

> the royal brothers of Portugal and Congo were writing letters to each other that were couched in terms of complete equality of status. Emissaries went back and forth between them. Relations were established between Mbanza and the Vatican. A son of the Mweni-Congo was appointed in Rome itself as bishop of his country.[6]

This bishop, Dom Henrique, had studied in Lisbon, and when he led a delegation of Congo noblemen to Rome for his consecration, he addressed the pope in Latin.

Nzinga Mbemba, baptized as Dom Afonso, was a truly extraordinary man. I have written of him elsewhere, but want to emphasize that he learned in middle life to read and speak Portuguese. It was said that when he examined the legal code of Portugal he was surprised by its excessive harshness. In jest he asked the Portuguese envoy what the penalty was in his country for a citizen who dared to put his foot on the ground! This criticism was probably reported back to the king of Portugal, for in a 1511 letter to his 'royal brother', Dom Afonso, he made defensive reference to differing notions of severity between their two nations.[7] Can we today imagine a situation in which an African ruler is giving, rather than receiving, admonition on law and civilization?

The Christian kingdom of Dom Afonso I in Congo did not fare well and was finally destroyed two centuries later after a long and protracted struggle with the Portuguese. A major source of the problem was the determination of the Portuguese to take out of Congo as many slaves as their vast new colony in Brazil demanded, and the Congo kings' desire to limit or end the traffic. There was also a dispute over mining rights. In the war that finally ended the independence of the kingdom of Congo and established Portuguese control over it, the armies of both nations marched under Christian banners.

If this story reads like a fairy tale, that is not because it did not happen but because we have become all too familiar with the Africa created by Conrad's *Heart of Darkness*, its long line of predecessors going back to the sixteenth century, and its successors today, in print and the electronic media. This tradition has invented an Africa where nothing good happens or ever happened, an Africa that has not been discovered yet and is waiting for the first European visitor to explore it and explain it and straighten it up, or, more likely, perish in the attempt.

In Conrad's boyhood, explorers were the equivalent of today's Hollywood superstars. As a child of nine, Conrad had pointed at the center of Africa on a map and said: When I grow up I shall go there! Among his heroes were Mungo Park, who drowned exploring the River Niger; David Livingstone, who died looking for the source of the Nile; Dr Barth, the first white man to approach the gates of the walled city of Kano. Conrad tells a memorable story of Barth 'approaching Kano which no European eye had seen till then', and an excited population of Africans streaming out of the gates 'to behold the wonder'.[8]

And Conrad also tells us how much better he liked Dr Barth's first-white-man story than the account of Sir Hugh Clifford, British governor of Nigeria, traveling in state to open a college in Kano, forty years later. Even though Conrad and Hugh Clifford were friends, the story and pictures of this second Kano event left Conrad 'without any particular elation. Education is a great thing, but Doctor Barth gets in the way.'[9]

That is neatly and honestly put. The Africa of colleges is understandably of little interest to avid lovers of unexplored Africa. In one of his last essays, 'Geography and Some Explorers', Conrad describes the explorers he admired as 'fathers of militant geography', or even more reverentially as 'the blessed of militant geography'. Too late on the scene himself to join their ranks, did he become merely a militant conjurer of geography, and history? Let it be said right away that it is not a crime to prefer the Africa of explorers to the Africa of colleges. There were some good people who did. When I was a young radio producer in Lagos in the early 1960s, a legendary figure from the first decade of British colonial rule in Nigeria returned for a final visit in her eighties. Sylvia Leith-Ross had made a very important study of Igbo women in her pioneering work *African Women*, in which she established from masses of personal interviews of Igbo women that they did not fit European stereotypes of downtrodden slaves and beasts of burden.[10] She graciously agreed to do a radio program for me about Nigeria at the turn of the twentieth century. It was a wonderful program. What has stuck in my mind was when she conceded the many good, new things in the country, like Ibadan University College, and asked wistfully: 'But where is my beloved bush?'

Was this the same hankering for the exotic which lay behind Conrad's preference for a lone European explorer over African education? I could hear a difference in tone. Sylvia Leith-Ross was gentle, almost self-mocking in her choice, and without the slightest hint of hostility. At worst, you might call her a starry-eyed conservationist! Conrad is different. At best, you are uncertain about the meaning of his choice. Until, that is, you encounter his portrait, in *Heart of Darkness,* of an African who has received the rudiments of education:

> And between whiles I had to look after the savage who was fireman. He was an improved specimen; he could fire up a vertical boiler. He was there below me and, upon my word, to look at him was as edifying as seeing a dog in a parody of breeches and a feather hat walking on his hind legs. A few months of training had done for that really fine chap. He squinted at the steam-gauge and at the water-gauge with an evident effort of intrepidity – and he had filed teeth too, the poor devil, and the wool of his pate shaved into queer patterns, and three ornamental scars on each of

his cheeks. He ought to have been clapping his hands and stamping his feet on the bank, instead of which he was hard at work, a thrall to strange witchcraft, full of improving knowledge.[11]

This is poisonous writing, in full consonance with the tenets of the slave trade – inspired tradition of European portrayal of Africa. There are endless variations in that tradition of the 'problem' of education for Africa; for example, a highly educated African might be shown sloughing off his veneer of civilization along with his Oxford blazer when the tom-tom begins to beat. The moral: Africa and education do not mix. Or: Africa will revert to type. And what is this type? Something dark and ominous and different. At the center of all the problems Europe has had in its perception of Africa lies the simple question of African humanity: are they or are they not like us?

Conrad devised a simple hierarchical order of souls for the characters in *Heart of Darkness*. At the bottom are the Africans, whom he calls 'rudimentary souls'. Above them are the defective Europeans, obsessed with ivory, petty, vicious, morally obtuse; he calls them 'tainted souls' or 'small souls'. At the top are regular Europeans, and their souls don't seem to have the need for an adjective. The gauge for measuring a soul turns out to be the evil character Mr Kurtz:

He had the power to charm or frighten rudimentary souls into an aggravated witch-dance in his honor, he could also fill the small souls of the pilgrims with bitter misgivings – he had one devoted friend at least and he had conquered one soul in the world that was neither rudimentary nor tainted with self-seeking.[12]

The alleged tendency of Africans to offer worship to any European who comes along is another favorite theme in European writing about Africa. Variations on it include the veneration by Africans of an empty Coca-Cola bottle that falls out of an airplane. Even children's stories are not free of this insult, as I once learned from foolishly buying an expensive, colorful book for my little girl without first checking it out.

The aggravated witch-dance for a mad white man by hordes of African natives may accord with the needs and desires of the fabulists of the Africa that never was, but the experience of Congo was different. Far from falling over themselves to worship their invaders, the people of this region of Africa have a long history of resistance to European control. In 1687, an exasperated Italian priest, Father Cavazzi, complained:

These nations think themselves the foremost men in the world. They imagine that Africa is not

only the greatest part of the world, but also the
happiest and most agreeable . . . [Their king] is
persuaded that there is no other monarch in the
world who is his equal.[13]

Between Father Cavazzi's words and Joseph Conrad's
images of gyrating and babbling savages there was
indeed a hiatus of two harsh centuries. But that would
not explain the difference.

People are wrong when they tell you that Conrad was
on the side of the Africans because his story showed
great compassion towards them. Africans are not really
served by his compassion, whatever it means; they ask
for one thing alone – to be seen for what they are: human
beings. Conrad pulls back from granting them this favor
in *Heart of Darkness*. Apparently, some people can read it
without seeing any problem. We simply have to be
patient. But a word may be in order for those last-ditch
defenders who fall back on the excuse that the racial
insensitivity of Conrad was normal in his time. Even if
that were so, it would still be a flaw in a serious writer – a
flaw which responsible criticism today could not gloss
over. But it is not even true that everybody in Conrad's
day was like him. David Livingstone, an older contem-
porary and by no means a saint, was different. Ironically,
he was also Conrad's great hero, whom he placed

among the blessed of militant geography . . . a notable European figure and the most venerated perhaps of all the objects of my early geographical enthusiasm.[14]

And yet his hero's wise, inclusive humanity eluded Conrad. What did he think of Livingstone's famous judgment of Africans?

I have found it difficult to come to a conclusion on their [Africans'] character. They sometimes perform actions remarkably good, and sometimes as strangely the opposite . . . After long observation, I came to the conclusion that they are just a strange mixture of good and evil as men are everywhere else.[15]

Joseph Conrad was forty-four years *younger* than David Livingstone. If his times were responsible for his racial attitude, we should expect him to be more advanced than Livingstone, not more backward. Without doubt, the times in which we live influence our behavior, but the best or merely the better among us, like Livingstone, are never held hostage by their times.

An interesting analogy may be drawn here with the visual arts imagery of Africans in eighteenth-century Britain. I refer to a 1997 exhibition at the National

Portrait Gallery in London on the subject of Ignatius Sancho, an eighteenth-century African man of letters, and his contemporaries. The centerpiece of the exhibition was the famous painting of Ignatius Sancho by Thomas Gainsborough in 1786. The art historian Reyahn King describes the painting in these words:

> Gainsborough's skill is clearest in his treatment of Sancho's skin colour. Unlike Hogarth, whose use of violet pigments when painting black faces results in a greyish skin tone, the brick-red of Sancho's waistcoat in Gainsborough's portrait, combined with the rich brown background and Sancho's own skin colour, makes the painting unusually warm in tone as well as feeling. Gainsborough has painted thinly over a reddish base with shading in a chocolate tone and minimal colder lights on Sancho's nose, chin and lips. The resulting face seems to glow and contrasts strongly with the vanishing effect so often suffered by the faces of black servants in the shadows of 18th-century portraits of their masters.[16]

Evidently Gainsborough put care and respect into his painting; and he produced a magnificent portrait of an African who had been born on a slave ship and, at the time of his sitting, was still a servant in an English aristocratic household. But neither of these facts was allowed to take away from him his human dignity in Gainsborough's portrait.

There were other portraits of Africans in Britain painted at the same time. One of them provides a study in contrasts with Gainsborough's rendering of Ignatius Sancho. The African portrayed in this other picture was one Francis Williams, a graduate of Cambridge, a poet, and a founder of a school in Jamaica: an amazing phenomenon in those days.[17] A portrait of Williams by an anonymous artist shows a man with a big, flat face lacking any distinctiveness, standing in a cluttered library on tiny broomstick legs. It was clearly an exercise in mockery. Perhaps Francis Williams aroused resentment because of his rare accomplishments. Certainly the anonymous scarecrow portrait was intended to put him in his place, in much the same way as the philosopher David Hume was said to have dismissed Williams's accomplishments by comparing the admiration people had for him to the praise they might give 'a parrot who speaks a few words plainly'. It is clear, then, that in eighteenth-century Britain there were Britons, like the painter Gainsborough, who were ready to accord respect to an African, even an African who was a servant; and there were other Britons, like the anonymous painter of

Francis Williams, or the eminent philosopher Hume, who would sneer at a black man's achievement. And it was not so much a question of the times in which they lived as the kind of people they were. It was the same in the times of Joseph Conrad a century later, and it is the same today!

Things have not gone well in Africa for quite a while. The era of colonial freedom which began so optimistically with Ghana in 1957 would soon be captured by Cold War manipulators and skewed into a deadly season of ostensible ideological conflicts which encouraged the emergence of all kinds of evil rulers able to count on limitless supplies of military hardware from their overseas patrons, no matter how atrociously they ruled their peoples.

With the sudden end of the Cold War, these rulers or their successor regimes lost their value to their sponsors and were cast on the rubbish heap and forgotten, along with their nations. Disaster parades today with impunity through the length and breadth of much of Africa: war, genocide, military and civilian dictatorships, corruption, collapsed economies, poverty, disease, and every ill attendant upon political and social chaos! It is necessary for these sad conditions to be reported, because evil thrives best in quiet, untidy corners. In many African countries, however, the local news media cannot report these events without unleashing serious and even deadly consequences. And so the foreign correspondent is frequently the only means of getting an important story told, or of drawing the world's attention to disasters in the making or being covered up. Such an important role is risky in more ways than one. It can expose the correspondent to actual physical danger; but there is also the moral danger of indulging in sensationalism and dehumanizing the sufferer. This danger immediately raises the question of the character and attitude of the correspondent, because the same qualities of mind which in the past separated a Conrad from a Livingstone, or a Gainsborough from an anonymous painter of Francis Williams, are still present and active in the world today. Perhaps this difference can best be put in one phrase: the presence or absence of respect for the human person.

In a 1997 calendar issued by Amnesty International USA in a joint effort with the International Center of Photography, a brief but important editorial message criticizes some current journalistic practices:

> The apocalyptic vision of the newsmakers [does not] accurately document the world community. Nor are they particularly helpful in forming a picture of our common humanity.[18]

And the text goes on to set down the principles which guided the selection of the twelve photographs in the calendar, as follows:

> [They] document an authentic humanity. They also communicate the fact that every person, everywhere, possesses an inalienable rightness and an imperishable dignity – two qualities that must be respected and protected.[19]

There is a documentary film which I have seen more than once on PBS which is not troubled by Amnesty's concern. It is about sex and reproduction through the entire range of living things, from the simplest single-cell creatures in the water to complex organisms like fishes and birds and mammals. It is a very skillful, scientific production that pulls no punches with respect to where babies come from. It is all there in its starkness. Was it necessary to conclude this graphic reproductive odyssey with man (or rather woman)? I did not think so. The point had already been more than well made with apes, including, I believe, those that invented the 'missionary position.'

But the producers of the documentary were quite uncompromising in their exhaustiveness. And so a woman in labor *was* exposed to show the baby coming out of her. But the real shock for me was that everybody in that labor room was white except the Ghanaian (by her accent) mother in childbirth. Why were all the rest white? you may ask. Because this was all happening in a hospital in London, not in Accra.

I am sure that the producers of that program would reject with indignation any suggestion that their choice of candidate was influenced in any way by race. And they might even be right, to the extent that they would not have had a meeting of their production team to decide that a white woman would not be an appropriate subject. But then, such deliberations do not happen except perhaps in the crude caucuses of the lunatic fringe. Race is no longer a visible presence in the boardroom. But it may lie, unseen, in our subconscious. The lesson for that production team, for those who broadcast their product, and for the rest of us is that when we are comfortable and inattentive, we run the risk of committing grave injustices absentmindedly.

1998

Africa Is People

I believe it was in the first weeks of 1989 that I received an invitation to an anniversary meeting – the twenty-fifth year, or something like that – of the Organisation for Economic Co-operation and Development (OECD), in Paris. I accepted without quite figuring out what I could possibly contribute to such a meeting/celebration. My initial puzzlement continued right into the meeting itself. In fact it grew as the proceedings got under way. Here was I, an African novelist among predominantly Western bankers and economists; a guest, as it were, from the world's poverty-stricken provinces at a gathering of the rich and powerful in the metropolis. As I listened to them – Europeans, Americans, Canadians, Australians – I was left in no doubt, by the assurance they displayed, that these were the masters of our world, savoring the benefits of their success. They read and discussed papers on economic and development matters in different regions of the world. They talked in particular about the magic bullet of the 1980s, structural adjustment, specially designed for those parts of the world where economies had gone completely haywire. The matter was really simple, the experts seemed to be saying: the only reason for failure to develop was indiscipline of all kinds, and the remedy a quick, sharp administration of shock treatment that would yank the sufferer out of the swamp of improvidence back onto the high and firm road of free-market economy. The most recurrent prescriptions for this condition were the removal of subsidies on food and fuel and the devaluation of the national currency. Yes, the experts conceded, some pain would inevitably accompany these measures, but such pain was transitory and, in any case, negligible in comparison to the disaster that would surely take place if nothing was done now.

Then the governor of the Bank of Kenya made his presentation. As I recall the events, he was probably the only other African at that session. He asked the experts to consider the case of Zambia, which according to him had accepted, and had been practising, a structural adjustment regime for many years, and whose economic condition was now worse than it had been when they began their treatment. An American expert who seemed to command great attention and was accorded high deference in the room spoke again. He repeated what had already been said many times before. 'Be patient, it will work, in time. Trust me' – or words to that effect.

Suddenly I received something like a stab of insight and it became clear to me why I had been invited, what I was doing there in that strange assembly. I signaled my desire to speak and was given the floor. I told them what I had just recognized. I said that what was going on before me was a *fiction workshop*, no more and no less! Here you are, spinning your fine theories, to be tried out in your imaginary laboratories. You are developing new drugs and feeding them to a bunch of laboratory guinea pigs and hoping for the best. I have news for you. Africa is not fiction. Africa is people, real people. Have you thought of that? You are brilliant people, world experts. You may even have the very best intentions. But have you thought, *really* thought, of Africa as people? I will tell you the experience of my own country, Nigeria, with structural adjustment. After two years of this remedy, we saw the country's minimum wage plummet in value from the equivalent of fifteen British pounds a month to five pounds. This is not a lab report; it is not a mathematical exercise. We are talking about someone whose income, which is already miserable enough, is now cut down to one-third of what it was two years ago. And this flesh-and-blood man has a wife and children. You say he should simply go home and tell them to be patient. Now let me ask you this question. Would you recommend a similar remedy to your own people and your own government? How do you sell such a project to an elected president? You are asking him to commit political suicide, or perhaps to get rid of elections altogether until he has fixed the economy. Do you realize that's what you are doing?

I thought I could read astonishment on some of the faces on the opposite side of the huge circular table of the conference room. Or perhaps it was just my optimistic imagination. But one thing I do know for a fact. The director-general (or whatever he was called) of the OECD, beside whom I was sitting, a Dutchman and quite a giant, had muttered to me, under his breath, at least twice: 'Give it to them!'

I came away from that strange conference with enhanced optimism for the human condition. For who could have imagined that in the very heart of the enemy's citadel a friend like that Dutchman might be lurking, happy enough to set my cat among his own pigeons! 'Africa is people' may seem too simple and too obvious to some of us. But I have found in the course of my travels through the world that the most simple things can still give us a lot of trouble, even the brightest among us: and this is particularly so in matters concerning Africa. One of the greatest men of the twentieth century, Albert Schweitzer – philosopher, theologian, musician, medical missionary – failed completely to see the most obvious fact about Africa and so went ahead to say: 'The African is indeed my brother, but my junior brother.' Now, did we or did anyone we know take Dr Schweitzer up on that blasphemy? Oh no. On the contrary, he was admired to the point of adoration, and Lamberene, the very site on African soil where he uttered his outrage, was turned into a place of pilgrimage.

Or let us take another much admired twentieth-century figure, the first writer, as it happens, to grace the cover of the newly founded *Time* magazine. I am talking, of course, about that extraordinary Polish-born, French-speaking English sea captain and novelist, Joseph Conrad. He recorded in his memoir his first experience of seeing a black man in these remarkable words:

> A certain enormous buck nigger encountered in Haiti fixed my conception of blind, furious, unreasoning rage, as manifested in the human animal to the end of my days. Of the nigger I used to dream for years afterwards.[1]

My attention was first drawn to these observations of Conrad's in a scholarly work, not very widely known, by Jonah Raskin. Its title was *The Mythology of Imperialism*, and it was published in 1971 by Random House. I mention this because Mr Raskin's title defines the cultural source out of which Conrad derived his words and ideas.

Conrad's fixation, admitted so openly by him in his memoir, and conspicuously present in his fiction, has gone largely unremarked in literary and scholarly evaluations of his work. Why? Because it is grounded quite firmly in that mythology of imperialism which has so effectively conditioned contemporary civilization and its modes of education. Imperial domination required a new language to describe the world it had created and the people it had subjugated. Not surprisingly, this new language did not celebrate these subject peoples nor toast them as heroes. Rather, it painted them in the most lurid colors. Africa, being European imperialism's prime target, with hardly a square foot escaping the fate of imperial occupation, naturally received the full measure of this adverse definition. Add to that the massive derogatory endeavor of the previous three centuries of the Atlantic slave trade to label black people, and we can begin to get some idea of the magnitude of the problem we may have today with the simple concept: *Africa is people.*

James Baldwin made an analogous point about black people in America, descendants of Africa. In his essay 'Fifth Avenue, Uptown', he wrote:

> Negroes want to be treated like men: a perfectly straightforward statement containing seven

45

words. People who have mastered Kant, Hegel, Shakespeare, Marx, Freud and the Bible find this statement impenetrable.

The point of all this is to alert us to the image burden that Africa bears today and make us recognize how that image has molded contemporary attitudes, including perhaps our own, to that continent.

Do I hear in my mind's ear someone sighing wearily: 'There we go again, another session of whining and complaining!'? Let me assure you that I personally abhor and detest whiners. Those who know me will already know this. To those who don't, I recommend a little pamphlet I wrote at a critical point in my country's troubles. I called it *The Trouble with Nigeria*, and it is arguably the harshest statement ever made on that unhappy country. It is so harsh that whenever I see one of the many foreign critics of Nigeria quoting gleefully from it I want to strangle him! No, I am not an apologist for Africa's many failings. And I am hardheaded enough to realize that we must not be soft on them, must never go out to justify them. But I am also rational enough to realize that we should strive to understand our failings objectively and not simply swallow the mystifications and mythologies cooked up by those whose goodwill we have every reason to suspect.

Now, I understand and accept the logic that if a country mismanages its resources it should be prepared to face the music of hard times. Long ago I wrote a novel about a young African man, well educated, full of promise and good intentions, who nevertheless got his affairs (fiscal and otherwise) in a big mess. And did he pay dearly for it!

I did not blame the banks for his inability to manage his finances. What I did do, or try to do, was offer leads to my readers for exploring the roots of the hero's predicament by separating those factors for which an individual may justly be held accountable from others that are systemic and beyond the individual's control. That critical, analytical adventure to which the book invites its readers will be medicine after death for my hero, but the reader can at least go away with the satisfaction of having tried to be fair and just to the doomed man, and the reward, hopefully, of a little enlightenment on the human condition for himself.

The countries of Africa (especially sub-Saharan Africa) on whom I am focusing my attention are not the only ones who suffer the plight of poverty in the world today. All the so-called Third World peoples are, more or less, in the same net, as indeed are all the poor everywhere, even in the midst of plenty in the First and Second Worlds.

Like the unfortunate young man in my novel, the poor of the world may be guilty of this and that particular fault or foolishness, but if we are fair we will admit that nothing they have done or left undone quite explains all the odds we see stacked up against them. We are sometimes tempted to look upon the poor as so many ne'er-do-wells we can simply ignore. But they will return to haunt our peace, because they are greater than their badge of suffering, because they are human.

I recall watching news on television about fighting in the Horn of Africa, between Ethiopia and Eritrea. As I had come to expect, the news was very short indeed. The only background material the newscaster gave to flesh out the bald announcement of the fight was that Ethiopia and Eritrea were among the world's poorest nations. And he was off, to other news and other places, leaving me a little space and time to mull over the bad news from Africa. How much additional enlightenment did that piece of information about poverty give the viewer about the fighting or the fighters? Not much. What about telling the viewer, in the same number of words, that Eritrea was a province of Ethiopia until recently? But no. The poverty synecdoche is more attractive and less trouble; you simply reach for it from the handy storehouse of mythology about Africa. No taxing research required here.

But if poverty springs so readily to our minds when we think about Africa, how much do we really know about it?

In 1960 a bloody civil war broke out in Congo soon after its colonizer, Belgium, beat a hasty retreat from the territory. Within months its young, radical, and idealistic prime minister, Patrice Lumumba, was brutally murdered by his rivals, who replaced him with a corrupt demagogue called Mobutu, whose main attraction was presumably his claim to be an anti-communist. Mobutu set about plundering the wealth of this vast country, as large as the whole of Western Europe, and also fomenting trouble in Congo's neighboring countries, aiding and abetting the destabilization of Angola and openly cooperating with the apartheid white-minority regime in South Africa. Mobutu's legacy was truly horrendous. He stole and stashed away billions in foreign banks. He even stole his country's name and rebaptized it Zaire. Today Congo, strategically positioned in the heart of Africa, vast in size and mineral wealth, has also become one of the poorest nations on earth. Whom are we to hold responsible for this: the Congolese people, Mobutu, or his sponsors, the CIA? Who will pay the penalty of structural adjustment? Of course, that question is already irrelevant. The people are already adjusted to grinding poverty and long-range instability.

Congo is by no means the only country in Africa to have foreign powers choose or sustain its leader. It is merely the most scandalous case, in scale and effrontery.

President Clinton was right on target when he apologized to Africa for the unprincipled conduct of American foreign policy during the Cold War, a policy that scorched the young hopes of Africa's independence struggle like seedlings in a drought. I have gone into all this unpleasant matter not to prompt any new apologies but to make all of us wary of those easy, facile comments about Africa's incurable poverty or the endemic incapacity of Africans to get their act together and move ahead like everybody else.

I cannot presume to tell world bankers anything about public finance or economics and the rest. I have told you stories. Now let me make a couple of suggestions.

In the late 1990s an organization in Britain called Jubilee 2000 informed me of their noble campaign to persuade leaders of the world's rich nations (the G8 countries) to forgive the debts owed them by the world's fifty poorest nations. I was made to understand that the British government was half persuaded that it should be done, and that the Canadians were possibly of the same view. But, on the negative side, I learned that Japan and Germany were adamantly opposed to the proposal. About the most important factor, America, my informant had this to say: 'When asked about cancellation their tongues speak sweetly, like some of Homer's Greeks, but their hearts are closed. It needs another poet to go to them and lay siege to those hearts . . . will you be that poet?' Subsequently, my wife, noticing perhaps my anxiety, showed me a passage in a book she happened to be reading. 'The fact that a message may not be received is no reason not to send it.' I was startled by the message and the mystery of its timely surfacing. I also recognized the affinity between this thought and another I knew, wearing its proverbial Igbo dress: 'Let us perform the sacrifice and leave the blame on the doorstep of the spirits.' That's what I have now done.

Regarding Japan and Germany, beneficiaries both of postwar reconstruction assistance, I did not appeal to their hearts but instead nudged their memories and their sense of irony. And for good measure I told them the parable of Jesus about the servant who was forgiven a huge debt by his master, on leaving whose audience he chanced upon a fellow servant who owed him a very small sum of money. The first servant seized him by the throat and had him tortured and thrown into prison.

My second request to the World Bank went to the very root of the problem – the looting of the wealth of poor nations by corrupt leaders and their cronies. This crime is compounded by the expatriation of these funds into foreign banks, where they are put into the service of foreign economies. Consequently the victim country is defrauded twice, if my economics is correct: it is defrauded of the wealth which is stolen from its treasury and also of the development potential of that wealth forever.

In asking the World Bank to take a lead in the recovery of the stolen resources of poor countries, I did not suggest that such criminal transactions are made through the World Bank. I am also aware that banks are not set up normally to act as a police force. But we live in terrible times when an individual tyrant or a small clique of looters in power can destroy the lives and the future of whole countries and whole populations by their greed. The consequences of these actions can be of truly genocidal proportions.

Herein lies the root of the horrifying statistic to which the president of the World Bank, James Wolfensohn, drew attention: 'You will be staggered to know, as I was, that 37 percent of African private wealth is held outside Africa, whereas for Asia the share is 3 percent and for Latin America it is 17 percent.'[2]

It would be a great pity, I remarked, if the world were to sit back in the face of these catastrophic statistics and do nothing, merely to preserve codes of banking etiquette and confidentiality formulated for quite other times. The world woke up too late to the inadequacy of these codes in the matter of the Nazi Holocaust gold. We had thus been warned. The cooperation of the world's banks, led by the World Bank Group, in eliminating this great scourge would have given so many poor countries the first real opportunity to begin afresh and take responsibility for their development and progress, and it would have discouraged future marauders of nations. It would also have cleared the world's banking systems of the charges of receiving stolen property and colluding with genocide.

For too long the world has been content to judge peoples and nations in distress largely on the basis of received stereotypes drawn from mythologies of oppression. In 1910, at the height of British imperial dominion, John Buchan, a popular novelist who was also a distinguished imperial civil servant, published a colonialist classic entitled *Prester John*, in which we find the following pronouncement: 'That is the difference between white and black, the gift of responsibility.'

I do not believe such a difference exists, except in the mythology of domination. Let's put this to the test by giving these poor, black nations the first sporting chance of their lives. The cost is low and the rewards will blow our minds, white and black alike. Trust me!

Let me round this up with a nice little coda. 'Africa is people' has another dimension. Africa believes in people, in cooperation with people. If the philosophical dictum of Descartes 'I think, therefore I am' represents a European individualistic ideal, the Bantu declaration '*Umuntu ngumuntu ngabantu*' represents an African communal aspiration: 'A human is human because of other humans.'

Our humanity is contingent on the humanity of our fellows. No person or group can be human alone. We rise above the animal together, or not at all. If we learned that lesson even this late in the day, we would have taken a truly millennial step forward.

1998

Notes

Africa's Tarnished Name

1. Dorothy Hammond and Alta Jablow, *The Africa That Never Was: Four Centuries of British Writing about Africa* (Prospect Heights, Ill.: Waveland Press, 1992), pp. 22–23.

2. Joseph Conrad, *Heart of Darkness*, ed. Robert Kimbrough (New York: Norton, 1972), p. 37.

3. Ibid.

4. Ibid., p. 4.

5. I am indebted to Basil Davidson's *The African Slave Trade* (Boston: Little, Brown and Company, 1980) for the outline of this story.

6. Mbanza was the capital of the kingdom of Congo; the king soon renamed it São Salvador. The quoted passage is from Davidson, *The African Slave Trade*, p. 136.

7. Ibid., p. 152.

8. Joseph Conrad, 'Geography and Some Explorers,' *National Geographic* (March 1924).

9. Davidson, *The African Slave Trade*, p. 147.

10. Sylvia Leith-Ross, *African Women: A Study of the Igbo of Nigeria* (London: Faber and Faber, 1938); see p. 19.

11. Conrad, *Heart of Darkness*, pp. 38–39.

Notes

12. Ibid., p. 51.

13. Davidson, op. cit., p. 29.

14. Conrad, *Heart of Darkness,* p. 147.

15. David Livingstone, *Missionary Travels,* quoted in Hammond and Jablow, *The Africa That Never Was,* p. 43.

16. Reyahn King et al., *Ignatius Sancho: An African Man of Letters* (London: National Portrait Gallery, 1997), p. 28.

17. Ibid., p. 30.

18. William F. Schultz and Willis Hartshorn, '1997 Amnesty International Calendar: Photographs from the Collection of the International Center of Photography' (New York: Universe Publishing, 1996).

19. Ibid.

Africa Is People

1. Quoted in Jonah Raskin, *The Mythology of Imperialism* (New York: Random House, 1971).

2. James D. Wolfensohn, *Africa's Moment* (Washington, D.C.: The World Bank, 1998).